Peace in the Midst of Pain

Peace in the Midst of Pain

A Biblical Perspective on Pain and Suffering

Alice M. McGhee

iUniverse, Inc.
New York   Bloomington

Peace in the Midst of Pain
A Biblical Perspective on Pain and Suffering

iUniverse books may be ordered through booksellers or by contacting:

iUniverse
1663 Liberty Drive
Bloomington, IN 47403
www.iuniverse.com
1-800-Authors (1-800-288-4677)

ISBN: 978-1-4401-2336-8(pbk)
ISBN: 978-1-4401-2337-5(ebk)

Printed in the United States of America
iUniverse rev. date: 5/14/09

Acknowledgments

Thanks to Greg Smith of Littleton, CO for the design of the cover of this book. Thanks also for putting up with my "mind changes."

My daughters-in law, Armene' McGhee and Jeanne McGhee were invaluable help in proof-reading and sharing opinions.

My deepest thanks goes to my husband, Ken. I could not have finished this project without his "picky proofreading" and abundant encouragement.

DEDICATION

I have observed how Pastor Arnie Hamil demonstrated by his life how to live in the presence of his own personal pain. He has always had the attitude that pain did not give him an excuse for bitterness. He has never allowed his own pain to block his view of the pain others were suffering. Pastor Arnie has been a true inspiration to me.

Table of Contents

DEDICATION VII

PREFACE - I DON'T LIKE TO HURT XI

FALLING TO PIECES 1

WHAT A FRIEND WE HAVE IN JESUS 2

THE "P" FACTOR 5

GOD, DO YOU HEAR ME? 8

HIDDEN UNDER A LEAF 11

JOSEPH'S CUP OF LEMONADE 15

DADDY'S ARMS 19

REJOICE IN SUFFERING ? 21

THE PAIN BLANKET 23

PICKING UP THE PIECES 27

GOD'S LOVE MESSAGE TO ME 28

A SMALLER SLICE OF LIFE 30

REALITY? 33

A STRAIGHT BUT PAINFUL PATH 35

NO STRINGS ATTACHED 38

NEVER A DISCOURAGING WORD 41

PAIN IS A PAIN 45

HOLD MY HAND 48

MY SPIRITUAL BRACE 50

SOCIETY OF THE HOSPITALIZED 52

RISING TO PEACE 55

DISCONNECTED BODY PARTS 56

FOOT IN MOUTH DISEASE 59

A BUNDLE OF POTENTIALITY 63

THE SLIPPERY SLOPE 65

GOD'S BIG PLAN 67

MIND CONTROL 71

SCARS VS. BEAUTY MARKS 74

PEACE BEYOND UNDERSTANDING 76

THE BEST IS YET TO COME 79

MORE THAN A CONQUEROR 81

THE MIDNIGHT CRY 83

ABC'S OF PAIN MANAGEMENT 87

NOTES 91

PREFACE

I DON'T LIKE TO HURT

The kind of pain that keeps you awake at night, makes it difficult to complete daily activities, and causes large muscle knots in various places on your body is just not fun. When I started having these symptoms, my doctor diagnosed my illness as fibromyalgia. We tried a number of medications both prescription and herbal and we could not find a thing that had an appreciable effect on the pain. We tried several different doctors. Finally one came up with a combination of medications that seemed to help. Well, that was great until I realized that one of the meds made me gain thirty pounds in about 6 months.

I tried a rheumatologist, which is an arthritis specialist. That was one of the wisest decisions I have ever made. He really had an understanding of the disease and was able to give me just the right combination of prescriptions to make me feel better than I had in years.

During my initial visit with the rheumatologist, he looked into my throat and asked, "How long have you had sleep apnea?" I vehemently replied, "I don't have sleep apnea!" Dr. Wilson (not his real name) said, "Oh, yes, you do. And you have it bad too."

I proceeded with the test for sleep apnea, only to find my rheumatologist knew what he was talking about. According to the test score, I had the worst score Dr. Wilson had ever seen. Apparently I stop breathing for as long as 60 seconds at a time often while sleeping. I was immediately introduced to the joys of sleeping with a CPAP machine and mask.

While the sleep apnea and the fibromyalgia stuff were going on I was also having problems with my back. It would appear that I inherited degenerative disc disease from my father and a couple other forms of arthritis to boot. I had a spinal fusion on my neck in 1994. Later in a four-year period I had four (4) spinal surgeries, one shoulder surgery, and one wrist surgery. My left wrist is waiting to be fixed, too. It however, has been pre-empted by other pressing surgeries. All of these surgeries are related to the effects of one form of degenerative arthritis or another.

I have tried spiritual healing, too. Many people have laid hands on me and prayed for my healing, but it hasn't happened. I have tried to figure out where God is in all of this. I have come to the conclusion that He is right where He has always been on His throne ruling the universe. That location is exactly where He should be!

Sometimes when we pray for things, God may or may not give

us exactly what we ask for. For a long time I prayed that I wanted God to use me any way he chose to do so and I would leave the choice up to him. Since I wasn't healed when people prayed for me, it was as if God said "Did you mean that prayer you prayed or not? Are you willing to put your body where your mouth is?" I had to really get serious with God and decide if I had meant what I had prayed.

Because I am not a biblical expert and I do attend church regularly, it was extremely imperative that I figure out just what God was trying to accomplish in my life. I need to find something to hold onto that would make it all worthwhile. I came across a verse in Psalms 119:71, "It was good for me to be afflicted, so that I might learn your decrees." Did I read that verse right? How could being afflicted with all these things that cause me pain be "good for me? God, it just doesn't make sense. I have got to understand it -- understand what it really means.

The verse said it was good so that I "could learn your decrees." "Decrees" is one of the words used in Psalms 119 to refer to God's Word. So I am supposed to learn God's Word by being afflicted. But have I? There must be a purpose in the pain.

Here are some things I have learned about God's Word through my affliction.

God is always with me in pain and weakness.

II Corinthians 12:10

God will never leave me.

Joshua 1:9

God has a purpose for my life.

Acts 20:24

God does not mean to harm me, but means His best for me.

Jeremiah 29:11

God had a purpose in the Apostle Paul's pain.

II Corinthians 12:7

God is my comfort in affliction.

Psalms 119:49&50

God hears my cry for help.

Psalms 22:24

The weak live by the power of God.

II Corinthians 13:4

If I need to use a wheelchair and can't walk, that is not the most important thing to God.

Psalm 147:10&11

Maybe I have learned a few things. Thank you, God for my affliction. It has helped me know You better.

Falling to Pieces

WHAT A FRIEND WE HAVE IN JESUS

What a Friend We Have in Jesus by Charles C. Converse is a favorite hymn of many. It's words have brought comfort to people too numerous to mention. One day as I was reading the words of the second verse it had nearly the opposite effect on me.

The first line says *Have we trials and temptations?* I feel like shouting, "Um, Yeah! I have been praying about this pain for quite some time now!" The next phrase says, *Is there trouble anywhere?* "It's me God, I'm down here!" There is trouble right here! A song is not "God-breathed" like Scripture is; however, many songs may contain scriptural truth

The next line of the song says, *We should never be discouraged.* What I "should" do and what I actually do may be two different things. To never, ever allow myself to be discouraged in the midst of constant pain is an awfully tall order. Jesus Christ was discouraged enough to ask that the "Cup be taken from him" (Matthew 26:39) in the Garden of Gethsemane if it was his Father's will.

I have often heard it said that never is a very long time. When I constantly feel pain day after day, hour after hour, minute after minute, second after second, there are times when I am not sure I can reach out and grasp the next unit of time. I am not sure if it is my mind or my body that fails to respond. Perhaps it is little of both.

I think this song is one of those "shoulda, woulda, coulda" things because it says we <u>should </u>never be discouraged. In an ideal world we shouldn't be discouraged, but this is not an ideal world. It just happens to be a very sinful one. As a sinner I get discouraged. I hate to admit it, but I don't always do exactly what I should.

The solution mentioned in the song is to *"take it to the Lord in Prayer."* I have prayed about my pain issue many times. Next the songster poses a rhetorical question. *Who will all our sorrows share?* I guess that line of the song doesn't say "take away," does it? It says <u>share.</u> The weight of a heavy load is divided when carried by two- even when that weight just happens to be pain.

Further down in the same verse of the song is the phrase, *"Jesus knows our every weakness."* If Jesus knows my weak areas, he knows when I need help carrying the load.

Maybe taking my problems to the Lord is a pretty logical solution.

I love the last line of the third verse. *"In his arms He'll take and shield thee-*

Thou will find a solace there." As toddler I played a game with my grandfather when he and Grandma were babysitting for me. Just before mom and Dad came to pick me up I would sit on Grandpa's lap and he would cover me up with his overcoat. I felt so warm and safe with his arms surrounding me. I knew nothing could hurt me in that warm, cozy place. Grandpa shielded me -- he was my solace -- my refuge.

I am trying to relate Jesus to Grandpa. He knows my weaknesses, my aches and pains, and He is ready to cuddle me up in His arms and keep me safe in his presence.

THE "P" FACTOR

One of the ways pain impacts my life is that when I go shopping I need to use a wheelchair because that old monster "Pain" gets to be more than I can handle. Using the chair makes shopping less stressful for both my husband and me. Without it Ken (my husband) feels like he has to stop to let me rest every few minutes. He also feels it is a necessity to watch my face for the tell-tale signs I am in pain and too stubborn to let him know. If we use the wheelchair, we just buzz through the mall and both of us are comfortable and relaxed. I accuse him of being "pushy" and he accuses me of ordering him around and we both have a great time. So what is wrong with this picture? The dreaded "P" factor enters in and tries its best to spoil our shopping trip.

You've never heard of the "P" factor? It does have several aliases, but that is only to allow it to sneak up on me when I least expect it. It usually starts out harmlessly by making us wonder "What if?" For me this usually comes in the form of my questioning, "What will happen if someone from church sees me in the wheelchair?" My patient husband wisely answers, "What do you think will happen"? He would have to throw it right back into my lap wouldn't he? I have to admit to myself I fear that my "friends" would think I was a "wuss" or a "baby."

If I truly think of my "friends" that way, what kind of friends would they be? My friends all know I have a problem that causes me a lot of pain, so what I need to do is let them be the friends to me they want to be. I need to allow them to reach out to me and not allow the "P" factor to enter our relationship when they see me in my chair. I need to give them credit for being the great friends they are.

What that "P" factor is, is nothing but Pride. I just want to be "normal" (whatever that is). I want to be like them. I had to laugh the other day when a friend told me that she wished she could be like me because I had such a great attitude. If she could only see me in my weak moments she would know what I am truly like. But then I guess we all have weak moments.

More than wanting to be "normal," I really want to be a woman God can use. There has been a part of me that has been afraid He couldn't use me if I was handicapped. I heard Joni Eareckson Tada speak at a conference a couple of months ago. She said one thing that really stuck with me. "There is a powerful appeal in writing from a suffering heart." She should know about that if anyone does. Joni has such a winsome personality and in spite of all she has been through, Joni is in a chair all the time and God has certainly used her.

Last summer God directed my Bible reading to Psalms 147:10,"*His pleasure is not in the strength of the horse, nor his delight in the legs of a man; the Lord delights in those who fear him, who put their hope in his unfailing love."* WOW!!! So if I read that verse correctly -- the ability to walk is not what pleases God. What really pleases God is the condition of my heart -- not the condition of my body! That is really good news. So perhaps it would be a good idea to replace the "P" factor with the "C" factor. "C" for confidence that is. Confidence in Christ not in myself.

GOD, DO YOU HEAR ME?

When I call the doctor's office or even a friend with a question or problem I expect an answer. Sometimes I need to leave a message on an answering machine or voice mail system. When this is necessary, I expect a call back within 24 hours. If a person is truly my friend, they will call back. I would do that for my friends.

Sometimes I get really upset and get on the "hot line" to God. I leave several messages on his heavenly "voice mail" and it appears that He just doesn't call me back. It seems that God is silent. I wonder if my prayers are even reaching Him. I feel as if I am in some kind of black hole or perhaps behind a wall that keeps me from God and God from me.

I think Mary and Martha must have felt that way when their brother Lazarus became deathly ill. The sisters had already done everything they knew how to do. Their last resort was to send for Jesus. If Jesus loved them as He said He did, surely he would come and heal their brother. They knew he wasn't more than a day's journey away. As the night went on, Lazarus grew worse. By morning Jesus had not come. Lazarus died the following day. Going through the usual stages of grief, Mary and Martha were sad and angry that their friend had not come to save their brother. (Read this story in John 11)

Upon Jesus arrival, He found that Lazarus had been dead and buried four days. He was first met by Martha, who greeted him with a reprimand for not having come sooner. Mary came and delivered the same reprimand. Then Jesus wept in sadness over the death of His friend, Lazarus. Mary and Martha took Jesus to the tomb. Jesus prayed and told His Heavenly Father in John 11:42, "I know that you always hear me, but this is for the benefit of the people standing here, that they may believe that you sent me." Then Jesus called for Lazarus to come forth and he did. Many of the people who saw what happened believed in Jesus.

That was a great victory for Jesus. During the 5 or 6 previous days, Mary and Martha wondered where Jesus was and if he had gotten the message. In today's language, they wondered if he had checked His voice mail or e-mail. When we don't get an answer back as soon as we expect it, the human thing is to think that God has forgotten us or that He is too busy or maybe He is angry with us. We forget that one of the possible answers to prayer is WAIT. That is a word we don't like when it comes from other humans, let alone from God.

Psalm 27:14 says very specifically, "Wait for the Lord; be strong and take heart and wait for the Lord." A good companion verse is Psalms 40 verse 1. "I waited patiently for the Lord; he turned to me and heard my cry." I can wait, but I don't usually do it very patiently. I had to wait 5 years for the baby we had been praying to adopt. I must admit there were a lot of times that I did not wait patiently at all. I do know that when I held that baby in my arms it was worth the wait, as frustrating as it had been times. God had a purpose in every minute of it. He has a purpose in your wait or in the silence, too. We may not understand the purpose, but that is where trust comes in. I do trust God more than anyone. He has never let me down!

HIDDEN UNDER A LEAF

There is something very cheery about plants. I have a lot of them in my home. My husband thinks the living room looks like a jungle. I have African violets in the south facing windows. How they enjoy that sunlight. They like just the right amount of water. African violets do not like wet toes, you know.

I even like plants so much that I plant artificial plants in the front yard during the winter. Velvety poinsettias adorn pots in front of the house at Christmas. People often wonder how I get them to grow in our rough Colorado winters, before they discover the beautiful plants are artificial.

In Colorado, we are going through a time of drought. During a normal year our lawns need to be watered almost daily in order to keep them green. Our lawn watering time is rationed to 15 minutes per sprinkler zone, twice each week. We Coloradoans really appreciate our flowers and plants.

My husband can count on buttering me up with a surprise gift of flowers any day at all. Flowers are a gift that is never the wrong size, style, or color. They are appropriate for every holiday

There were two men in the Bible who appreciated plants. They actually sought out their plants during times of depression. However, they didn't use the blooms to cheer them up. The men did not use their colorful petals to decorate their homes. They did not cook the roots for a suppertime bowl of soup. Both men sat under the plants and used them for shade and eventually slept under them. Have you guessed the names of these men? They were Elijah and Jonah.

We can read Elijah's story in I Kings 18 and 19. Elijah had just fought the prayer battle of the universe. The odds were 850 to 1. When that one is one plus God, it is a majority even if the other side is 850! God defeated the pagan gods Baal and Asherah in a prayer battle on Mount Carmel. Elijah was God's only representative. After God and Elijah's victory, Elijah had all the prophets of the false gods killed. The victory was complete. Jezebel, the Queen, was not happy that her prophets were killed or that her gods were proved useless. She put out a contract on Elijah's life. Instead of facing her like he did the prophets, Elijah ran for the desert. That is where he found his plant.

It was under this plant that we find Elijah telling God "'I've had enough. Just let me die! I'm no better off than my ancestors.' Then he laid down in the shade and fell asleep." Wait a minute. This is victorious Elijah? It sure is. And he wants to die? He is so depressed he is ready to die. He is feeling so alone and deserted by God that he doesn't care to live any more. Elijah thinks he is the only person in the world serving God. He has gone from a mountain top of great victory to a valley of great defeat. The defeat is still defeat, even if it is emotional or spiritual.

The other plant sitter was also depressed. Jonah had delivered God's message of repentance to the people of Ninevah. The citizens responded to God's call and repented of their sin. God decided not to destroy the city of Nineveh because of the change of their hearts. This should have been a great victory for Jonah. However, Jonah became upset with God for not destroying Nineveh, so he sat under the plant and pouted. Like Elijah, Jonah said, "It is better for me to die than to live." Jonah had come all this way to watch God destroy a city and it was not going to happen. Jonah was angry. So God sent a worm to eat the plant. The plant died and Jonah had nothing. (Jonah 4:10) Jonah was more worried over a little plant than over the lives of thousands of people living in the city of Nineveh.

Both Elijah and Jonah were so upset they were ready to die and they sought shelter under a plant. Jonah's focus was on the plant and not on God. Elijah's focus was on the contract Jezebel had on his life, his aloneness, and not on God. In both cases the plant was symbolic of the point of their focus. When Elijah's focus was on God, great things happened. The greatest prayer battle in history was won for God. When Jonah's focus was on God, the entire population of a great city experienced spiritual revival. When Elijah and Jonah focused on themselves tragedy struck. A large fish swallowed Jonah and Elijah ran away to hide in the dessert. They both enjoyed the company of themselves at a pity party.

A song has recently been written by Toby Keith with words saying," I wanna to talk about me. It's all about I. It's all about number 1!" When Jonah and Elijah were in the self-focused mind-set even a red rose would not have cheered them up! I am not sure that the plants had that much to do with their situation, but God used the plants as a way to help take some of the pressure off while still allowing them to work out their problems.

God revealed to Elijah that there were 7,000 others who still remained faithful to Him -- Elijah was NOT alone in serving God. Elijah moved on, took Elisha as his assistant and accomplished more great things for God. (I Kings 19:18-21)

Scripture doesn't say what happened to Jonah. I don't know if he moved his focus to God or kept it on the shriveled plant. If he kept it on the plant, he died a miserable individual.

There are times when I have wondered why I was alive. I have not crawled under a plant for shelter yet. The key lesson in this story is: "Where is my focus? Is it on my surroundings, my pain, or is it on God? As long as my focus stays on my Heavenly Father, I will have nothing to be depressed about and everything to rejoice about.

Plants or flowers may help to take my mind off myself. I may not use a plant for shelter, but my husband can buy me flowers any time he likes!

JOSEPH'S CUP OF LEMONADE

Parenting is one of the toughest jobs of all. There are many authorities, each with his own theory on the best way to get the job done. Most authorities disagree on techniques and methods, but they usually agree in one point -- don't favor one child over another. The problem of favoritism greatly increased the sibling tension you would expect in the family of the twelve boys we read about in the book of Genesis.

Jacob not only favored his second wife Rebekah, but he favored the child born to her in his old age, Joseph. Joseph is recorded as giving his father a "bad report" about his brothers (Genesis 37:2). This act on Joseph's part did not endear him in the hearts of his brothers. I am sure they viewed him as a "little tattletale." When their father gave Joseph a beautifully colored coat like none they had ever seen, it was obvious that their father, Jacob, loved Joseph more than any of the other brothers.

Joseph told his brothers about a dream he had where he and his brothers were in a field binding sheaves of wheat. The sheaves of all his brothers bowed down to his. In another dream the sun, moon, and eleven stars bowed down to Joseph. The brothers could hardly stand it. They grew to hate him more and more. They envied him for the place he had in their father's heart. (Genesis 37:11)

Most of the brothers were out watching the sheep. Jacob sent Joseph to see how the brothers were doing. When the brothers saw him coming, they decided to do something to get him out of their lives for good. Some wanted to kill him, but Reuben convinced them to throw Joseph into a pit. They took Joseph's beautiful coat. A caravan was on its way to Egypt. They sold Joseph to the merchants as a slave. What a change to go from favored son to slave.

The brothers tore his coat of many colors so it looked as if an animal had attacked Joseph. Then they killed the kid of a goat and dipped the coat in its blood. They returned the damaged and bloody coat to their father. Jacob was convinced Joseph had been killed by a wild animal.

I can't imagine Joseph's pain, to be taken from his home and family to a country where he didn't even speak the language. Joseph had lived a life of privilege and now he had been bought by Potiphar, the captain of Pharaoh's guard, just like a piece of pottery.

Joseph didn't understand why all this was happening, but he determined that he was going to do his best at what ever he was given to do. Eventually, he was in charge of Potiphar's household. Then he was put in prison because of a lie. He worked so hard in the prison and was so trustworthy; he became the equivalent of a trustee in the prison. While there he interpreted the dreams of a couple of inmates and both of their dreams came true.

When one of those inmates was out of prison and working for the Pharaoh, he heard that Pharaoh had a dream no one could interpret. The servant told Pharaoh about Joseph in prison.

Pharaoh called for Joseph to be brought to him. Joseph said he could only tell Pharaoh what his God told him. God gave Joseph the interpretation of the dream. Joseph told the Pharaoh of Egypt how he could prepare for a great famine that would come in seven years. There would first be seven years of plenty. During that time they should save up grain, so that they would have enough during the following seven years of famine.

The Pharaoh was so impressed with Joseph that he made him second in command in the country of Egypt. Joseph was in charge of the grain storage so there would be enough for the famine years. The king saw great wisdom in him.

Much grain was stored during the years of plenty. So much that the Egyptians could sell grain to those who were in need. One day a family of eleven brothers came to buy grain for their families in Canaan. Joseph knew who they were, but accused them of being spies. He said one brother would need to remain behind in Egypt until they returned with their younger brother Benjamin to prove their identity. When they began to run out of grain again, the brothers convinced Jacob to allow Benjamin to return to Egypt with them.

On the return trip, Joseph invited the brothers to have dinner with him. The brothers noticed that their seats were mysteriously arranged from oldest to youngest. They couldn't figure out how Joseph would know their birth order. When Joseph came in, He broke into tears, and identified himself as their lost brother.

Joseph sent the brothers to Canaan to get Jacob and their wives and children. They all moved to Egypt so they could be together. The Pharaoh of Egypt instructed Joseph to give them property in the land of Goshen as their own.

After Joseph's family arrived in their new home, he reassured them that they didn't need to fear him. Even though Joseph suffered greatly at their hands, he was no longer resentful of them. In Genesis 50:20 we read that Joseph could look back and see that what his brothers "meant for evil, God meant for good."

At the time the difficult things were happening, Joseph led a very painful life. It was obvious that he tried to "make lemonade out of lemons" through everything. At many junctures Joseph could have chosen the natural route to become consumed with hate, bitterness, ill-will, and anger. Joseph even chose to add sugar to his "lemonade." He did more than just "go with the flow." Joseph chose to be a man God could use even though his living conditions were not what he might choose them to be. We have that same choice to make. When our living conditions are challenged by financial hardship, illness, or loss of a job, will we suck on sour lemons or make lemonade with sugar? God can use us in spite of ourselves if we yield to His control. The choice is ours.

DADDY'S ARMS

It is a good thing my body parts are not fastened together with glue because some days the pain is so bad I would positively come UNGLUED! I don't think super glue or epoxy would be strong enough.

I just hate the scale of 1-10 the therapists and nurses always give you as a means of evaluating your pain. "10" is supposed to be the worst pain possible and zero is no pain at all. I have been known to tell them "12 or 15" after a particularly painful test. On those days, pain is the dominant factor in my life. There is no eating, sleeping, running errands, reading -- only existing. Heat will aid occasionally. Sometimes the pain pills take the edge off, but if I resort to pills then I sacrifice clarity of thought. On these days I just want to scream. What would feel really good would be for someone to wrap me in a blanket, cuddle me in their arms, and rock me to sleep in a big comfy chair. Singing Broadway show tunes softly would be nice, too. My husband could accomplish all those feats, but the Broadway show tunes might be a stretch. I would like to be coddled like a little baby for a while.

One of my grandchildren is approaching his first birthday. He gets all the loving, rocking, singing, and cuddling he wants whether he is in pain or not. I guess we all have to grow up, but that "baby-type lovin'" would feel pretty great even to a grown up now and then.

When I am feeling like every cell and hair follicle in my body is rubbed raw, I can read Zephaniah 3:17. *"The Lord your God is with you, he is mighty to save. He will take great delight in you, he will quiet you with his love, he will rejoice over you with singing."* God is my Abba Father (Romans 8:15), my spiritual Daddy who can wrap me up in the blanket of His love. The verse says He will take "great delight" in me. I can't understand how anyone could delight in me when I am in such a state. It is not for me to understand. It is for me to believe. *"I have loved you with an everlasting love."* *(Jeremiah 31:3)*

When my nerves are raw and screaming the Zephaniah 3:17 verse says that God will "quiet me with his love." That means God will give me those loving cuddles that will ease my jangled nerves and calm my troubled spirit. God will give me the T.L.C. or tender loving care that will make me give a great big sigh of relaxation. Then God will rejoice over me with singing. I think the singing will probably more likely resemble an angelic choir than Broadway show tunes.

That list covers everything I said I needed to settle me down during my worst bouts of pain. I will still take my pain pills. But I know they will be more effective and work faster when I rest in my Abba "Daddy's" arms.

REJOICE IN SUFFERING ?

"Rejoice in sufferings"? Did I read that right? I read that in Romans 5:3. My immediate reaction is to say, "I don't think so." Suffering is no fun. The Apostle Paul of all people should know that. He was stoned, whipped, shipwrecked, and imprisoned. I don't imagine he was thrilled about any of those experiences. But to actually "rejoice" or be happy in suffering is almost too much to ask. The Greek word translated "rejoice" can also be translated "boast, glory, or joy."

We need to read what is on the other side of the conjunction "because" in order to get the reason why we are to "rejoice" in our sufferings. The next phrase says "suffering produces patience or perseverance." A friend used to have a plaque in her kitchen, which she had embroidered. On the plaque was a cannon with red, white, and blue sparkles shooting out of its mouth. The words printed on it said, "Lord, give me patience and give it to me now!"

My friend's plaque indicated she wanted the patience or perseverance without the suffering. It would be nice, if you could get patience as a gift, but it doesn't come that way -- it needs to be earned or learned. It definitely doesn't come gift- wrapped.

Suffering was a daily occurrence for the first century Christian. Facing persecution was the "game" they played. They did not enjoy the suffering with which they were forced to live, but they knew God would use it to build their character. We find challenges each and every day that stretch our patience or perseverance. The more times we are challenged, the more times we can look back and see how God led us through hard times in previous days. It does get easier to transfer that thought to the future and say "if God could help me in the past, I know He can help me today and tomorrow."

The fact that I can envision God helping me tomorrow is the stuff from which hope is made. Hebrews 11:1 defines hope as believing in something you can't see. I can't reach out and touch God like the disciples did. I can see and feel the result of His work in my life. My attitude about myself and about being able to trust in God has changed dramatically since I took the risk to trust in that One I could not see.

We can look at God's Word, the Bible, even though it was written a long time ago, to give us future hope. Romans 15:4, *"For everything that was written in the past was written to teach us, that through endurance* (patience or perseverance) *and encouragement of the Scriptures we might have hope."* It may be a struggle to rejoice in the actual suffering, but I can definitely rejoice in the hope to come!

THE PAIN BLANKET

Many people do not understand the nature of chronic pain. The dictionary describes "chronic" as meaning "continuing for a long time; a disease of long duration." Most folks think that when you go to a doctor and get medication that the disease should be gone. Chronic pain is just made more manageable or "livable" with medication. It doesn't go away.

I just had my sixth back surgery for degenerative disc disease. After every single surgery people have said something like, "Now your surgery is over. Aren't you glad you won't have any more pain or surgery?" What my friends seem to have difficulty grasping is the fact that I may have had a surgery and my recovery is going right on schedule or even ahead of schedule. However, it doesn't mean that I will have no more pain or surgery as the result of degenerative disc disease. All it means is that the present diseased site is fixed. I will feel well until another disc bulges and then herniates or explodes. Usually it seems that I run one to two years between spinal surgeries. One of the frustrating parts is trying to convince my doctors, I have yet another "problem" when it does occur. When it is so bad there is numbness in my arms or legs from compressed nerves, the doctors have to do something.

The chronic part of the illness resembles a circle that just keeps going 'round and 'round. Sometimes I feel like a hamster on one of those exercise wheels who desires to jump off with all his heart but is unable to.

My chronic pain is caused by something deep within my body that cannot be seen. I don't wear a bandage on it or a brace (most of the time). I look perfectly healthy. If I have a smile on my face, it is difficult to know that anything is physically wrong with me. People are often amazed to discover that I am in pain.

There are several ways I cover up my pain. My favorite "pain cover-up blanket" is a sense of humor. It is very difficult to gripe, complain, and laugh at the same time. I have tried and cannot do those three all at once. Proverbs 17:22 says "A cheerful heart is a good medicine, but a crushed spirit dries up the bones." With my disc problem, I certainly don't need dry bones.

The next "pain cover-up blanket" is the old change the subject trick. When people approach me and want to know how I feel and I sense they really don't want to know how I feel. I ask them how they feel or mention the pastor's sermon or the weather.

The best and most successful "pain cover-up blanket" is to get my mind on the need of another person. In fact, we are instructed in Galatians 6:2 to "Carry each other's burden's, and in this way you will fulfill the law of Christ." It seems to me, that the more I think about myself, the more I draw inside myself and become depressed. If I can just keep my thoughts from getting too internal, it really helps me emotionally and physically. Being in a better mood eases my muscle tension. Eased muscle tension helps me relax and that helps a lot of things.

Using a "pain cover-up blanket" helps me deal with my pain better. It also helps people feel more comfortable around me and able to treat me like a "normal" person.

Picking Up the Pieces

Alice M. McGhee

GOD'S LOVE MESSAGE TO ME

I felt as if I were in the bottom of a deep, dark pit. My arms were extended upward reaching for my Heavenly Father, but He seemed just out of my reach. I had been in Christian counseling to help me deal with physical and emotional abuse in my past that had left me like a broken piece of china that was no good for anything.

I was having one of those days when everything that could go wrong did go wrong. As I watered my houseplants, I knocked one off onto the floor. It made an awful mess. The pot broke and there was dirt everywhere. I picked up the pieces of broken terra cotta trying to be sure I didn't cut myself when I heard a still small voice speak to me from inside my heart. I knew it had to be God. I had been waiting for Him to talk to me. He said, "I want you to get some glue and glue the pieces of the broken pot together." This made no sense at all to me. The pot was probably worth about 50 cents. But I obeyed the still, small voice. I looked at the finished creation. There were holes where the pieces didn't fit together just right and I was never very good at jigsaw puzzles. Now what, God? My answer came quickly. "Put a plant in it." Why pot a plant in a cracked pot? God, I don't understand. God spoke to my spirit and reminded me that His ways were not always my ways. (Isaiah 55:8) So, I followed instructions. The African violet I put in the pot looked great, but the pot had definitely seen better days.

I asked God to please explain to me what this whole "cracked pot thing" was supposed to mean for me. God said, "Alice, my child, you are like the pot. A little damaged and you might have a few flaws. But you see, my love is the glue that holds your broken pieces together. Just as that beautiful African violet will grow just fine in that broken cracked pot, you are still a useable vessel for me. I can use you in my service even if you have a few flaws." That cracked pot was my rope out of the pit!

I love reading in the Bible about Peter, Paul, Martha, and John Mark because they had flaws or "cracks" just like me. God was able to love and use them just the same!

A SMALLER SLICE OF LIFE

A certain amount of security goes along with knowing what to expect. When our kids were growing up we always tried to prepare them for new situations. That first visit to the dentist could be a scary thing until we let them know that the dentist always gives stickers or toys to good patients.

Our oldest son had allergies and asthma. He did not like the idea of taking allergy shots. The wise doctor had a system where each time the kids got a shot they got a star on a card. That card was used similar to a bank. The patients could "buy" toys from a cabinet when they had "saved" up enough stars. Some days he wanted to get a shot when it wasn't even time just so he could get a star on his card.

While in most cases knowing what to expect is a good thing, sometimes it can work in reverse. Once a person has major surgery and knows how long it takes to get through the recovery, including the physical therapy, the individual is very hesitant to have major surgery again. A person who has had previous back surgery can wait until they risk permanent nerve damage before they agree to have a second surgery because they know all that is involved.

My husband has encouraged me to use a Day Timer to help me keep track of appointments and tasks I need to do each day. The forgetfulness of "fibro-fog" that comes with fibromyalgia makes it necessary to have some sort of plan to keep track of things. Sometimes I feel discouraged just looking at my day to day activity plan. The pain level of the fibromyalgia keeps me on the couch some days and the plan gets shelved. That does nothing but put the whole week's plan off by a day. I feel very guilty when I get behind schedule.

AA, or Alcoholics Anonymous, is famous for their emphasis on taking "One day at a time." Whether the AA people realize it or not the "One day at a time" advice is very Scriptural. If we read Jesus own words in the Sermon on the Mount in Matthew 6:34, we are told not to "worry about tomorrow, for tomorrow will worry about itself." It just seems that if I look to the things of tomorrow I have tomorrow's things as well as today's to worry about. I think one day's worth of worries is enough to deal with at a time.

There have been times when I can really identify with the last part of verse 34. "Each day has enough trouble of its own." Some days appear to actually have too many troubles of their own. The troubles of some days seem virtually overwhelming.

When I feel overwhelmed by the troubles of a day, I find it helpful to take the day in small slices. To think about taking that "one day at a time" is too much. Maybe I need to just deal with a couple of hours at a time. If that is too overwhelming take a smaller slice, perhaps one hour, or only a half hour. Getting through life in small manageable chunks really helps. When I have successfully dealt with that small chunk, I deal with the next one. This method works whether the problem is depression or physical pain. Dealing with life in small chunks is a technique that can be an aid in facing a difficult situation. The "small chunk" method is far superior to trying to ignore the situation.

Whether a day turns out to be a bitter pill or a sweet treat, it must be swallowed. Each day should be dealt with one at a time because that is the plan Jesus gave us. Why should we do it His way? According to Matthew 7:29, "…he (Jesus) taught as one who had authority." Jesus had the authority to tell us how to do things. If we are obedient to His authority, today and every other day will work out better.

REALITY?

A person can hardly watch TV these days without running into some type of "reality" show. I put "reality" in quotation marks because sometimes I wonder about their definition of reality. You can see everything from a group of people stranded on a desert island to a group of people living in a house in California.

The groups of people on a reality show go through various forms of deprivation. The deprivation may range from doing without water for several days- to eating nothing but peanut butter and jelly for a week. The contestant's degree of commitment may be tested by whether or not they can eat grubs and various insects. Part of the pain they all have to undergo is separation from their families and other loved ones.

Various tricks are played on the contestants just to play with their minds. Anything the organizers of the shows can do to cause conflict is done because they think it will make a more "interesting" show. The more fights and disagreements they can cause -- the better. It is all in the interest of THE GAME.

What comes out in these reality games is how selfish the competitors are. The closer it gets to the end of the game, the more ruthless the competitors become. The lying and back-stabbing increases. All they can think of is the million dollar prize. There can be only one winner. The rest will all be losers. No matter how well they have played the game, all but one will be losers. They will suffer the pain of defeat.

There is a "prize" we can strive for in Philippians 3:14. That prize is mentioned back in verse 12 as being something "I press to take hold of that for which Christ Jesus took hold of me." In other words, we can work for it, but Christ has already given it to us. The prize is spelled out in verse 10 -- "to know Christ and the power of his resurrection and the fellowship of sharing in his suffering, becoming like him in his death and so, somehow, to attain to the resurrection from the dead."

To "press on" (verse 14) means to focus on the goal and run toward it. In this competition there are no losers. Yes, I said no losers. There will be no pain of defeat at this finish line. Everyone that Christ has "taken hold of" is already in the winners' circle. Jesus is waiting at the finish line to award everyone a blue ribbon (their prize). More specifically, the prize is going to Heaven as He has called us to do (Philippians 3:14).

What we will encounter in Heaven is truly reality. There will be no tears there (Revelation 7:17). We will walk on streets of gold (Revelation 21:21). The gates are made of pearls (Revelation 21:21). Lamps will not be needed because "The Lord God will give them light" (Revelation 2:5). This is not a game. One of the best parts is that there will not be any pain at all (Revelation 21:4). The best thing of all is to be in the presence of Jesus Himself. This will be true REALITY.

A STRAIGHT BUT PAINFUL PATH

Dave Dravecky had had surgery on his upper arm for cancer. He was making an unbelievable comeback as a pitcher in major league baseball. Everything was going well. Dave was hopeful. The day came when everyone on the field heard the snap as his arm broke while he pitched the ball. Dave could not believe the pain. He could not believe the news that the cancer had spread. Not only would it be necessary to amputate his arm, but his shoulder as well. Dave's baseball career was over. After the initial shock wore off, he summed up his feelings as follows: *"he (God) is a loving parent who is determined to bring us to maturity. He will use suffering in his children's lives in the same way a sculptor uses a chisel. As the craftsman of the human soul, God knows best which edges need to be smoothed and where fine lines must be etched to bring out the true beauty of his creation. He loves us too much to allow us to remain trapped in our rough, stony state. Thus, he may use pain and suffering to shape our lives and transform our character."*

God has used pain in the lives of Dave Davecky and his wife, Jan, to encourage many. He travels now and does motivational seminars, always giving glory to God for bringing him through a dark time in his life. God definitely used "pain and suffering to transform his character." God continues to use this baseball player in amazing ways other than on the baseball field.

God used a little Jewish girl in amazing ways. She was an orphan who was raised by her cousin. In many ways she was just like any other Jewish orphan, but God had set her apart for he had a special job for her to do and it was not without pain.

After living in the palace in Susa for a year's preparation, Esther won the Miss Susa Beauty Pageant. There was something about her heart or her spirit that made her stand out from all the other beautiful women. She was chosen to marry King Xerxes. Her cousin and guardian, Mordecai, cautioned her to keep her Jewish heritage a secret.

Haman, who was second in the kingdom to Xerxes, was infuriated because Mordecai, the Jew, refused to bow down to him when he walked through the city gate. Haman even had it made a law that everyone must bow down when he walked through the gate. Of course, Mordecai would bow down to no one but God. So Haman hated all Jews and decided to get rid of them. He got the king to sign a law stating that on a certain day all Jews would be killed.

Because of Esther's sheltered life in the palace, she was unaware of the new law until Mordecai brought it to her attention. Esther realized that all the Jewish people in the country were scheduled to be slaughtered -- including her. Mordecai told her that the fate of her people rested in her hands. In Esther 4:14 Mordecai told Esther, "…who knows but that you have come to royal position for such a time as this?" I can see Esther saying that she can't do it. I can also picture Mordecai telling her that God can.

I can't imagine the pain she suffered as she looked forward to her own death as well as that of her people. She put her life on the line when she approached King Xerses to invite him to dinner. At the dinner she invited him to another dinner the following day. The next day he asked her what she wanted, and she begged King Xerxes for her life and the lives of her people. Xerxes ordered Haman killed for his genocidal law and the Jews were allowed to defend themselves. Persian laws could not be changed.

God used a little Jewish girl in spite of her nervousness and pain. She didn't know why she won the Miss Susa pageant. Esther had no idea why her parents were killed. She was greatly saddened to grow up as an orphan. She was frightened to put her life on the line for her people in approaching the king without being called. She did not understand everything, but she was willing to trust God. Proverbs 3:5&6 -- "*Trust in the Lord with all your heart and lean not on your own understanding; in all your ways acknowledge him and he will make your paths straight.*" Neither Esther nor Dave Dravecky understood the "means to the end." However, by acknowledging God, they could see Divine planning at work, once they got near the end.

NO STRINGS ATTACHED

I felt violated as the juvenile jail guard repeatedly ran his fingers through my hair and asked me where the metal object was. Most of the jail personnel were dressed in casual street clothes, but I got "Rambo." The guard checking me into the visitation area was dressed in camouflage pants with the legs of the pants stuffed into his high-topped boots. This was complimented with a khaki-colored t-shirt. "Rambo" was convinced I was trying to smuggle something into the jail. He ran his fingers through my hair to see if I had hidden contraband. He found nothing around the neck area of my clothing because I had already removed my jewelry as required. I tried to explain to "Rambo" that I had had surgery and a metal plate and screws had been placed in my neck. He didn't believe me because he could see no scar on the back of my neck. I told him the scar was on the front of my neck and showed him where it was. He "wanded" me again. He finally decided to let me into the jail to see my son since he could not figure out any explanation for the beeping of his wand, but I knew he would be watching me.

That was by far the worst of the check-in experiences I had while going to visit my son while he did his time in the juvenile jail. He was there for drug possession and a lot of probation violations. He just could not accept the right of anyone to have authority over him whether it was legal, spiritual, parental, or social.

He was in a medium-security facility, which meant it was not a fun place to be. It is a hard thing to be a Christian parent and go to a place like that to visit your child every Sunday afternoon. The first thing my husband and I did was try to figure out where we went wrong. His probation and parole officers both said we had done everything by the book. We knew we had made some mistakes in parenting him, but an awful lot of the mistakes were just plain his choice.

Sometimes it is hard to understand how living in a sinful world can touch our Christian children, even in spite of our prayers. Satan is the Prince of this World (John 12:31). He tricked Eve to disobey God right in the perfect Garden of Eden. (Genesis 3:1-6) From the point in history where Eve and Adam sinned in the Garden of Eden, the rest of us have had to deal with living in a sinful world. Sometimes our children choose to make the choice of Adam and Eve -- disobedience, as many of us once did. However, I John 4:4 tells us "...the one who is in you is greater than the one who is in the world." God will give us the strength to stand up to Satan if we choose to do so, but we must make that choice.

One of the greatest pains a parent can feel is when a child makes a mistake that will hurt himself or another. As parents we do have a responsibility to teach our children "the way they should go" (Proverbs 22:6). When they reach a point where they know the difference between right and wrong, (that may come at a later age for some than others), we as parents need to let the consequences of their actions take over. When the consequences hurt them, they hurt us. It is difficult to see your son led off in handcuffs and shackles. It places a hurt in a parent's heart like nothing else.

As I prayed one day, I told God He had no idea what it felt like to have his child turn against him and say he hated him. Then my own words stopped me in my tracks. God knows exactly what it feels like to have his children turn against him. The children of Israel did it many, many, times. Being realistic, I have not been all I could have been for God. But, joyfully, He still loves me!

Unconditional love is what we read about in Psalms 103:12, "as far as the east is from the west, so far has he removed our transgressions from us." Loosely paraphrasing, Romans 5:8, it means that God didn't come here from Heaven to save us because we were perfect people, but because we were sinners who needed him.

I have not been in jail like my son has. I have felt great pain because he was there. I missed him and I wished he didn't have to be there. But I knew that when we adopted him we were stewards of his life. His being in jail was God's way of taking over the parenting responsibilities because we couldn't handle it. It didn't mean that God loved him or us any less. In fact it was a sign of how unconditionally God did love him. Through it all my husband and I learned how to love our son with no strings attached just like God did.

NEVER A DISCOURAGING WORD

I live in the state of Colorado in the area that was actually referred to as "The Range." Originally, the Ute Indians led by Chief Colorow inhabited this area. After the Meeker Massacre the Ute Indians were "relocated" to the Uintah Reservation on the Utah-Colorado Border. Sometime later Major R.B. Bradford had a large ranch in the area just outside of what was beginning to be the boomtown of Denver. The most famous owner of the property was John C. Shaffer who purchased it in 1914. He developed the property until it became a 10,000 acre cattle ranch. John Shaffer was a lavish entertainer. Some of his more famous guests included President William Howard Taft, President Theodore Roosevelt, and Indian Princess Teianina. The old farmhouse has been turned into a gourmet restaurant, called The Manor House, where you can eat rattlesnake if you so choose.

Why all the history? I have been rather "taken" with the idea of the very place where my house sits having been "Range" at one time. Cattle ranged through my back and front yards. The old "Home on the Range" song put my mind in gear. There are many exciting sights and sounds here. It is not unusual to see a red fox run in front of your car. Small herds or families of elk and deer roam through the neighborhoods. I love to hear the chirping of the birds, especially in the spring time. There is something very pleasant and comforting about all the "natural" sights and sounds.

The old folk song "Home on the Range" describes this area to a "T", even though it became the Kansas state song. The song refers to "seldom a discouraging word" being heard on "The Range." Maybe that is the way it was back then, but that is not the way it is now. I have heard a "discouraging word" recently, Range or not. That discouraging word is SURGERY.

To some people, surgery might not seem too bad. In the last four years, I have had three spinal surgeries, one shoulder surgery, and a hand surgery. Just hearing that I needed another spinal surgery was enough to make my whole emotional being come unglued. I think a horseback ride on "The Range" might ease the tension, but then it would probably make the pain in my back a whole lot worse.

It is amazing how the mention of a single word can quickly take a person from happiness and laughter to sadness, tears, and on to depression. The emotional jump can take place in minutes or even seconds. This is the path of discouragement. It is a path or almost like a slippery water slide. It seems like once you are on the downward slope, it is very difficult to stop and turn around until you hit bottom and can go no farther down. The only way is up. The best way off the slippery slide is to never hop on in the first place.

I checked my favorite book of advice -- not Oprah, not Dr. Phil -- The Bible. In Joshua 1:9, we read, "I've commanded you to be strong and brave. Don't ever be afraid or *discouraged!* I am the Lord your God and I will be there to help you wherever you go."

Who is doing all the commanding in this verse? The Lord, God, that's who. He "commands" that I am not to be discouraged or afraid, ever. That is a big order for someone who lives "on the range" where discouraging words are "seldom to be heard." That means that even when I do hear a discouraging word, I can't let it discourage me. It is my choice to make.

At least God doesn't expect me to do it alone. He says in the same verse that He will be right there to help me. That is such a comfort to know that God will be here on "The Range" to comfort me, to keep me from getting discouraged.

God's presence is not confined to "The Range." Joshua 1:9 said God's presence would be with me "wherever I go." That means if I go to Alaska God is there; if I go to South America, God is there; if I go to China God is there. *Psalms 139:9-12 agrees. "Suppose I had wings like the dawning day and flew across the ocean. Even then your powerful arm would guide and protect me. Or suppose I said, 'I'll hide in the dark until the night comes to cover me over.' But you see in the dark because daylight and dark are all the same to you."*

I guess the fact that the skies here on "The Range" have been cloudy and rainy ALL day shows you can't run your life by an old song. However, you can run your life by the Bible. Its words are all true. I have found that God has truly been with me everywhere I have gone. He has always been there to comfort and help me.

Just as cloudy skies will come and go, so will discouraging words. When those discouraging words do come I need to let

Jesus help me not to have a discouraged spirit. Since I have heard that discouraging word, "SURGERY," lately, I have vowed with God not to have a discouraged spirit, but an uplifted one. I don't have to face the surgery alone. God has promised to be "with me wherever I go" -- even in the operating room!

PAIN IS A PAIN

I hate pain, because, well, pain is a PAIN. Webster's Dictionary defines pain as "A distressing feeling due to disease, bodily injury, or organic disorder." It also could be defined as "a distressing uneasiness of mind; grief." Somehow Webster missed the point. Pain is ever so much more than that. A person could not understand what pain is really like from reading his definition. I am not exactly sure how I would re-phrase it, but the definition does not give the reader any idea of the impact pain has on the life of a person. The dictionary idea of a "distressing feeling" does not even come close to the hurt a person feels who lives in pain. Pain can literally turn a person's life upside down.

When a person stubs his toe while getting a drink of water at night, it can cause a headache clear at the other end of the body. Persistent pain can cause a person's nerves to feel frayed and on the edge of depression. In extreme cases, suicide can be the result. Being in pain can cause tension in the muscles. This muscle tension can cause a stiff neck, a headache, or unexplained muscle pain.

Job was an Old Testament saint who seemed to have a pretty easy life. He was extremely wealthy, had a large family of 10 children, and many livestock. His character was exemplary. God pointed Job out to Satan during a meeting He was having with the angels. God identified Job as being a man who was "blameless, upright, who feared God and hated evil." Since Satan was an angel, he was qualified to be present. In Job 1:10, Satan challenged God by saying something to the effect that, "Of course Job is exemplary; you have protected him from everything bad." (paraphrase mine). Satan suggested in Job 2:5 that if God would strike Job's "flesh and bones" that Job would curse God to His face. I think what Satan figured was if God would cause Job to be in pain, that Job would curse God. Even Satan is aware of how life-altering pain can be.

God gave Satan permission to do anything to Job but take his life. The first thing Satan did was give Job horrible pain. Job was given sores from the "top of his head to the soles of his feet" (Job 2:7). Job's wife taunted him adding emotional pain to the physical pain he was already experiencing. She even encouraged Job to turn his back on God and die. In all this Job did not sin. He was a man of great integrity just like God said.

Job also suffered the emotional trauma over the death of all ten of his children. Briggands stole his cattle and livestock. To all appearances Job was a broken man.

In order to help, Job was visited by three of his friends. These so-called friends were sure Job had sinned, and "Job's great sin" was the reason God had sent these great judgments of pain and loss upon him.

Job's friends were well-meaning, but they were wrong. They were wrong as to the source of the pain and reason for it. In spite of their good intentions, they made Job's situation emotionally more difficult for him.

When none of Satan's dirty tricks could get Job to turn on God, God returned all his livestock and Mr. and Mrs. Job had 10 more children. Satan was defeated and God won.

Job's difficulties had nothing to do with Job's sin, much to the chagrin and surprise of his friends. Job came through this test with his integrity and character in tact.

There are several things we can learn from Job's example. Those of us with chronic pain, whether physical or emotional, must not use our pain as an excuse to sin. We must also maintain our integrity. There may be well-meaning friends who really want to help, but don't know how. We must be patient and teach them how to meet our needs, or give us help, if they genuinely desire to do so. If they are like Job's wife in suggesting we "curse God and die," perhaps we should strongly suggest that they help someone else. If they are misguided like Job's friends as to what is behind our pain, we need to do as God instructed Job near the end of the book and pray for them.

"Pain is a pain," but we cannot use pain as an excuse for poor behavior that would dishonor God and rob us of our own dignity and integrity. If Job can survive in spite of pain, so can we. God has promised in numerous Scripture verses that He will never leave us nor forsake us. He <u>does</u> keep His promises. (Joshua 1:9; Hebrews 13:5; Deuteronomy 31:6)

HOLD MY HAND

When we adopted our first son he had many fears until he felt a secure part of our family. One of the things that bothered him was being in a large group of people. He had a real fear of becoming separated from us. It would be necessary for him to either be held by one of us or at least hold one of our hands.

He was nearly four years of age at the time we adopted him. When he came to live with us, the world as he knew it ceased to exist. The three of us began building a new world for him. He lived in a new house, with new parents, new toys, and a new dog. These kinds of changes can only be made over time and with a great deal of difficulty.

My 35-year marriage began when my father placed my hand in the hand of my groom that day in August. Later in the ceremony my new husband placed a ring on the third finger of my left hand as a symbol that I belonged to him. Even though we have been married thirty-five years, I still, get a smile on my face every time our hands touch. A clasping of hands still brings a sense of security to my heart.

When I am in the hospital and our hands touch, somehow I know that everything is going to be OK. Even when I am under the influence of mind numbing drugs, the touch of my husband's hand makes me feel calm.

A rough day is made so much easier when a special friend drops by for a cup of tea and cares enough to just hold my hand and take the time to listen to what is going on. She may not have the perfect advice to fix the situation, but the fact that she is there holding my hand means so much.

We just can't reach out and touch God like we can those family members and friends we love. We humans feel more secure when we can put our trust in something or someone we can reach out and touch. We like to be able to hold the money in our hands to pay our bills at the end of the month. A lot of people have their vacations planned so they have hotel reservations made for each night of their trip before they have left home rather than leave it to "chance."

God has even made provision to hold our hands during those difficult times. He has given His promise that He will do so. We can count on Him because He never breaks a promise. "So do not fear, for I am with you; do not be dismayed, for I am your God. I will strengthen you and help you; I will uphold you with my righteous right hand" (Isaiah 41:13). If I could bring security to a fearful child by holding his hand, how much more can my Heavenly Father bring security and comfort to this anxious and fearful child by holding my hand.

MY SPIRITUAL BRACE

Many people collect things that bring them pleasure. My sister collects lighthouses. I collect angel figurines. My husband used to collect different types of barbed wire. I had a friend with so many teddy bears that she would go to schools and civic groups and do presentations about them. I have also heard of thimble, spoon, plate, and cup and saucer collections.

Due to my arthritis and all the surgeries I have had, I have begun a collection I never thought I would have. It is a brace collection. I have both a hard and soft collar from neck surgeries. There is an elastic strap to hold my arm next to my body left over from a shoulder surgery. I have a couple sets of carpal tunnel splints for each arm and a sling. I think that makes up most of the upper body devices.

This is not a collection of things that brings me pleasure. The items listed in the above paragraph have eased my pain some before surgery and some after surgery and some both. I do need to pull one out for use every once in a while. I have been delaying surgery on my left wrist due to back problems so it has become necessary to splint my wrist at night. I am well prepared. I just pull one from my collection.

My extensive brace collection contains three different low back braces. I also have two ankle braces, one of which is a "boot" that extends up to my knee. These different braces have provided invaluable help in propping up my weakened body. Had I not been willing to use them following surgery, proper healing would not have taken place. After sprains, the splints or braces greatly reduced pain.

There are many sorts of braces to prop up our physical bodies, but what happens when we have a weakness in our spirits? These weaknesses cannot be braced with plastic and Velcro. Psalms 27:14 has an excellent idea of what to do to prop up a weakened spirit. Turn to God. "Wait on the Lord; be of good courage, and He shall strengthen your heart; wait I say, on the Lord!" So in other words, let God brace up our spirits or strengthen our hearts. He is not made of plastic and Velcro, He is ever so much stronger and more dependable.

Just as my big plastic box of braces is always available when I have a pain and need their help, God is present and ready to help. "God is our refuge and strength, a very present help in trouble." (Psalms 46:1). This verse tells us not only will God give us strength and help, but he will provide us with a refuge. A refuge is a safe haven where the person in trouble will be cared for and have all their needs met.

Every time I fasten a brace on some part of my body, I will use it as a reminder of how God "braces" or strengthens my spirit.

SOCIETY OF THE HOSPITALIZED

In order to become a member of the Society of the Hospitalized a person must be sick or have some broken body part that is badly in need of repair. Membership in this society is reserved for a very elite group. Group members are definitely in need of encouragement, comfort, and pampering. There are several reasons why members of this lofty club need a "pick me up."

Food is not one of the most exciting things about a hospital stay, especially if you are on a liquid diet. When variety means different flavors of clear gelatin, don't expect a gourmet meal. Hospital food just doesn't taste like home.

The beds aren't like home either. They are enclosed in protective plastic covers. Those plastic covers serve a purpose; however, they crackle every time you roll over or move on the bed. The crackling alone could keep a patient awake all night.

Another interesting facet of hospital stays is the air conditioned gowns each and every patient has the privilege of wearing. The "one size fits all" feature is debatable. Either they don't cover enough or they hang to the floor. The only way to be truly covered while wearing one is to wear two. Wear one in the usual way and one backwards with the opening in the front so it acts as a robe. This arrangement makes sure all the important "secret" equipment in the back is kept hidden.

Among the many challenges of "doing time" in a hospital would be attempting to get sleep when the staff continues to wake the patient to get "vitals" throughout the night. The "vitals" would be a blood pressure check, temperature check, seeing if you have a pulse, and basically seeing if the patient is still "vital" or alive. The patient may be vital but he or she is certainly no longer asleep after all that.

The only way to be sure you get your meds on time is to play a little game called "Whose Team Are You On"? The object is to let the nurses think you are on their team while still being on the patient's team. Sometimes the nurses get really crabby patients who are difficult to care for and put the nurses in a bad mood for their other patients. Some patients "play the game" by flattering the nurses. While the nurses earn every bit of flattery they can get, a better approach would be to combine teams with the common goal of the healing and recovery of the patient. If patients truly appreciate all the nurses and aides do for them saying, "Thank you," once in a while will help to improve the atmosphere. After all, there are often too few nurses, for too many patients. Taking care of sick people can often be a thankless job.

Doctors and nurses are not new to the 21st century. During the first century, Luke was called the "Beloved Physician" in Colossians 4:14. Luke, the physician, even worked with the apostle Paul (Philemon 24). He had an itinerant practice, without the benefit of our modern hospital facilities. Luke had to carry all his equipment and medicines with him.

I don't enjoy spending time in the hospital, but when I need surgery, it's a pretty good place to go. I feel so blessed to have the hands of the Great Physician, Jesus Christ guiding the hands of my doctor.

Welcome to the club!

Rising to Peace

DISCONNECTED BODY PARTS

The human body has been referred to as a magnificent machine. It has its own electrical system. The heart is a pump that keeps the blood flowing through the body from birth to death and rarely needs repairs. It has its own thermostat that maintains a fairly constant temperature unless infection is present. The body even heals itself when little cuts or burns take place. In a crisis situation, the adrenalin gets pumping and the ordinary human body can accomplish tasks requiring superhuman strength, such as lifting a car. This body is able to do many things because it is a unit of many parts all working together for the good of the whole unit.

God planned for His church to function in a similar way. If each person in His church does the job God calls him to do the church will function smoothly. (Ephesians 4:11-13). If everyone decides to preach and no one sings in the choir the church body will not function smoothly. Each person needs to do his/her own job and let everyone else do the jobs that God has called them to do. If a person who is right-handed breaks his right wrist, he will need to learn to write with his left hand, at least for a while. His body learns to compensate for the weak part.

As I have recovered from surgery I have definitely felt like a "weak body part." Other members of the church body have done my jobs for, me or compensated for my weakness in order to further the good of the whole body. People from church have brought over meals, cleaned our house, done our laundry, and driven me places. Everyone has been so helpful and done everything in love.

I have often heard it said, "It is more blessed to give than to receive." I have greatly appreciated all my friends have done for me. But it has been difficult for me to accept their acts of kindness. I have felt a certain amount of guilt or unworthiness. Maybe I am feeling like that "weak body part" that I am right now. I almost feel like a "disconnected" body part. It wouldn't bother me a bit if someone else had a problem and I needed to take them a meal or do cleaning for them. I would be happy to do it. Why should I expect them to feel any different about doing it for me? The concept of the body works well. The stronger body parts help the weaker parts -- in this case me. At another time it might be someone else. The whole idea is that we work together.

I think part of the reason I feel badly about it is that I have to admit my own weakness and I don't like that idea at all. It is hard for me to admit the fact that I really do need help. What it boils down to is that I am probably thinking far too much about my own "little toe" body part and not nearly enough about the whole. There may be other "body parts" that are also hurting in one way or another, maybe more than I am. I need to get my focus off myself and onto another part of the body (someone else)

Perhaps I should take the advice of Hebrews 12:2. *"Keep your eyes on Jesus, who both began and finished this race we're in. Study how he did it. Because he never lost sight of where he was headed -- that exhilarating finish in and with God- he could put up with anything along the way; cross, shame, whatever. And now he's there, in the place of honor, right alongside God."* (The Message)

FOOT IN MOUTH DISEASE

The early church received an astronomical boost when the apostle Peter preached his famous sermon on the Day of Pentecost. On that day alone, about 3,000 people were added to the church (Acts 2:41). In the days immediately following, many more people became believers in Jesus Christ, miracles were done, property was held in common; and the needs of everyone were met. It is easy to look at Peter and be pretty awestruck with his oratorical skills. However, it wasn't Peter's skills that got the job done. It was God working through Peter, putting just the right words into his mouth.

One of the things that seems to draw me to reading Scriptures about Peter is that He did not always do things the way he did on the Day of Pentecost. There were some days when he just plain "blew it." Peter seemed to have a bad case of "foot in mouth disease," or to put it differently, engaging his mouth before he engaged his brain.

Just prior to Jesus' arrest in the Garden of Gethsemane, Peter and the other apostles could not stay awake as Jesus had asked them to do while Jesus prayed (Matthew 26:40). I am so much like Peter and the others. I hate to admit the number of times I have fallen asleep while praying or while reading my Bible just because I lost my focus.

The soldiers of the high priests then entered the garden. Judas, who betrayed Jesus with a kiss, led them there. Peter pulled out a sword from under his robe, and proceeded to cut off the ear of the high priest's servant, Malcus (John 18:10). I can't help but wonder why Peter even had a sword with him. Malcus was glad Peter's skill as a fisherman apparently did not extend to his ability to wield a sword.

The three-year ministry of Jesus and his disciples had always been one of peace and love not of violence. Jesus had prophesied that He would be killed in Jerusalem. His disciples did not want to believe he would die. Perhaps, Peter wanted to be sure he was prepared "just in case" any trouble came up – thus, the sword. Peter still had not truly grasped who Jesus was. Jesus took care of the "damage control." He touched the ear of Malcus and healed it completely (Luke 22:51) before allowing himself to be taken off by the soldiers.

Peter's worst "open mouth –insert foot" moment came shortly before Jesus death. While Jesus was going through the farce of a trial Peter denied that he knew Jesus, his Lord and Savior -- not once, but three times. Peter was probably afraid of what others would think of him. If Peter were connected with Jesus, he might also have been arrested. Yet, Peter, the ever curious one, wanted to know what was happening with Jesus, but he may have also been equally concerned about his own skin.

Once the rooster crowed, Peter remembered Jesus' prophecy. I imagine he felt as if he had been stabbed with a knife and felt the knife being twisted in his stomach. Jesus was taken through the courtyard. Their eyes locked and Peter wanted to die with embarrassment. Scripture says in Luke 22:62,"He went outside and wept bitterly." Here we have the "Big Fisherman" who has dissolved into tears. He may have been the biggest and strongest of the apostles and he "wept bitterly." In this case, Peter was weeping because he "blew it" and he "blew it badly." What Jesus had said had come true.

Peter was weeping with good reason. Sometimes we cry because we are in physical pain and sometimes because we are in emotional pain. In this case, Peter was in emotional pain because of conviction of sin. He felt guilty because of his lying about not knowing Christ, not once, but three times.

You might wonder what place this has in a book on pain. There are times when I am angry and resentful about my illness. That anger has caused me to act out and speak to those caring for me in unkind ways. Sometimes I have felt I have totally lost control of my life and/or my mouth because I have to do what everyone around me tells me to do. Take my pills. Do my therapy. It's time to rest. It's time for a blood sample -- even if it is 3:00 A.M. I let my pain and anger control my mind and mouth -- "open mouth, insert foot" just like Peter. I end up feeling guilty for my sin. Usually I dissolve into tears just like Peter.

I am so thankful God has a remedy. It doesn't come in the form of an elixir, a tissue, or a pill. It more closely resembles a "spiritual bar of soap." We can find the remedy in I John 1:9 in the Bible. "*If we confess our sins, he is faithful and just to forgive, and to cleanse us (or wash away) from all unrighteousness.*" All we need to do is to admit our sin to God; ask Him for forgiveness'; and He washes all the dirt of that sin away.

Those "foot in mouth" sins may not seem as "dirty" as murder or bank robbery. But sin is sin and the "remedy" must be taken in order for healing to take place.

A BUNDLE OF POTENTIALITY

Bill Gaither wrote a song for little people a few years back that has a big message for big people today. The song was called, "I Am a Promise." If there was ever a self-esteem building song, this is the one. One line of the song says, "I'm a great big bundle of potentiality." I used to remind myself of that line from the song when my kids were giving me a lot of grief on any particular day. I would say, " Remember, they have a lot of potential -- a whole bundle in fact."

Now that they have children of their own, I can see some of that "potentiality" realized. It brings so much joy to a mother's heart to see her children and grandchildren living for and loving Jesus. Scripture agrees with this mother's heart. "I have no greater joy than to hear that my children are walking in the truth." (III John 4) And yet in some members of the family we still see "potentiality." They know the truth, but are not walking in it.

Webster defines "potentiality" as the "state of being possible, not actual." In other words our "bundle of potentiality" is the "possible" in storage. When the "possible" is released from storage it becomes "actual" -- the real, honest-to-goodness thing (our children living for the Lord). The hard thing we parents need to figure out is how to untie the bundle and release or free the "potentiality."

Here's the painful part. We can't do it. Our kids have to do it for themselves. They have to untie the strings on the bundle because they want to. The best thing we as parents can do is pray. Notice I didn't say the "only" thing we can do is pray. That is because prayer should not be viewed as a last resort or an inferior weapon to use. It is definitely the BEST!

One other thing we can do is to love our kids unconditionally. "To love unconditionally," means that we love expecting nothing in return. The unconditional love has been hard for me as a parent. I have a tendency to think they should love me, send me birthday cards, and buy me gifts because of all I did for them. My last statement is a great example of "conditional" love. Love that has expectations is conditional. We need to give our kids enough breathing room to love us in the ways they feel comfortable and ready to love. I have grown to the point where I love unexpected phone calls. Maybe that is what makes them so good, I don't expect them.

We have these "bundles of potentiality" in our families. Sometimes we need to love them for their "potential" rather than what they are right now. God can help us to do that. Psalms 143:8 speaks to those of us who need help in knowing how to get the job done. "Let the morning bring me word of your unfailing love, for I have put my trust in you. Show me the way I should go for I will lift up my soul." God's love promises to be unfailing.

THE SLIPPERY SLOPE

I found out the real meaning of the term "slippery slope," and I do mean slippery on the way home from choir practice about 9:30 P.M. one night. One of our Rocky Mountain blizzards had started during practice. By the time we left the church, the roads were covered with black ice and visibility was very limited.

Traffic was slowing down ahead of me. I realized I was not going to be able to stop, so I steered my car to the shoulder. The car ran up a hill on the right side of the road and began spinning. It went down the hill and back onto the road. It spun across two southbound lanes of traffic and onto a grassy median. All I was aware of was spinning lights. The car crossed the median and the two northbound lanes of traffic, spinning in circles all the while. Then the car left the highway, went through a fence, across a paved bike path and 150 feet down into a ravine.

You might guess that I was on the road all by myself. Well, I wasn't. The road I was driving on was a limited access Colorado State highway. There were a lot of cars on the road many of which were, like myself, having trouble staying on the road. I wasn't aware of the car jerking, only the spinning lights. I prayed a few things during the Great Spin. The first thing was that I told God that if He was ready for me I was ready for Him. I was sure that I was going to die. I knew my eternal destiny was sure because I have a personal relationship with the Son of God, Jesus Christ.

I have never been so glad to be able to say that as that night. I asked God to keep me from hitting and injuring anyone.

My third prayer was that Jesus would be my driver.

Each of my three prayers was answered. Apparently, even though I was ready, Jesus wasn't ready for me. The car hit no other cars even though there were many around. Jesus took over at the wheel because when I went down the ravine the car went down backwards. The emergency personnel cannot figure out how I steered it down backwards without it rolling over.

The gas line ruptured. The floor of each passenger compartment was raised by the rocks I hit, except the section where I was sitting. The whole frame of the car was twisted. My only injury was a concussion where I hit my head on the top of the car. I have surgical metal implants in my spine. By going down the hill backwards, my back and neck had the most support possible instead of being whiplashed back and forth.

I saw God answer so many prayers that night. It took me a few days to get my emotions back together and realize how miraculously God had saved my life. The police officer who investigated the accident said that "most people who park that far from the road don't walk out. They are carried back by a funeral director." I know God saved me for a reason. I keep reading Jeremiah 29:11 (For I know I have a plan for you…) and praying that I will find and fulfill whatever is God's reason for saving me. I don't want my life to be a slippery slope, but a solid rock with a light on top shining for Jesus.

GOD'S BIG PLAN

There is nothing so pleasant and peaceful as a baby sleeping in his mother's arms. They are unaware of the wars in the world or the political situation. The baby completely trusts his mother to care for his needs. The mother is filled with such a sense of love for her baby. If it were called for, she would give her life to save that of her beautiful child's. This picture is one of rare serenity in our troubled world today.

It is expected that once a couple gets married they will eventually have children. This is assumed by nearly everyone. If children don't arrive within a few years, the mothers of the couple usually start asking when they will become grandmothers. Sometimes this ability to bare children is almost taken for granted. There are many couples who, for a variety of reasons, physically cannot give birth to children of their own.

This is especially difficult for the wife of the couple. It seems that God has put into the heart of most women a very strong desire to have children. When it is not possible, a part of the woman seems to be unfulfilled. Maybe a better way to state it would be it just seems something is missing from her life. Infertility has also been one of my struggles. Going to baby showers has often felt like adding insult to injury. Even people who knew my situation would forget and ask how long I had been in labor with one of my adopted sons. I used to say "5 years" because that is how long the adoption process took for our first son. The pain has eased some with time and I handle it more graciously than I used to, but the empty spot is still there.

I find it always helps to look at Scripture to see how to deal with any pain. In I Samuel Chapter 1 we read the story of Hannah. Hannah could not have children. In her culture it was doubly bad because she was view as "flawed" or "worthless" because she could not present her husband with sons. By not having sons it also meant that when she became a widow, she would become a pauper with no one to care for her. Hannah also had to deal with her husband's second wife, Peninnah. Peninnah was constantly taunting Hannah and making life miserable for her. Perhaps the reason her husband even had a second wife was Hannah's inability to have children.

On a trip to Shiloh to make their yearly sacrifice, Hannah went into the place of worship to pray. As she poured out her heart to God, tears filled her eyes and she began sobbing. Eli, the priest, thought she was drunk and rebuked her. She told Eli that she had not been drinking, but her heart was filled with sadness. Eli said "Go on your way, for the God of Israel will answer your prayer." As Hannah returned to her family group, she was filled with a new hope. She told God that if He answered her prayer for a son that she would give him back to serve God the rest of his life.

Some months later Samuel was born to Hannah and Elkanah. True to her promise, Hannah took Samuel to live with Eli the priest as soon as he was old enough to be weaned. God blessed

Hannah with other children. Each year during the yearly sacrifice trip Hannah would take Samuel a new linen coat.

Hannah knew the pain of not being able to have children. There were others in Scripture who did not have children until they were quite old; Sarah, the wife of Abraham and Elizabeth, the cousin of Mary. I don't understand it all, but I do know that God always has a plan. In my case, we adopted two sons. I know without a shadow of a doubt that God planned before the foundation of time for those two boys to be raised by my husband and myself. If we had been able to have children in the usual way we would probably not have been open to the idea of adoption. In God's plan we needed to parent those children.

There are many things about God I just don't understand. Isaiah 55:8, *For my thoughts are not your thoughts, neither are your ways my ways, declares the Lord."* So I guess according to that verse I can expect that there will be things I don't understand. Trust and Faith enter the game at this point. Part of the definition of faith in Hebrews 11:1 is "being certain of what we do not see." That sounds a lot like believing what I don't understand to me. Even when things still hurt and I don't understand all the whys, that is when I need to trust in God's love for me. I need to trust that when I don't understand The Plan, God does and will work out the details.

I often find listening to Christian music to be very comforting and soothing. One of my favorites is a song called "Trust His Heart" by Eddie Carswell and Babbie Mason (© Causing Change

Alice M. McGhee

Music and Dayspring Music - a div. of Word, Inc.). I especially like the chorus of the song. _God is too wise to be mistaken. God is too good to be unkind. So when you don't understand, when you don't see His plan, when you can't trace His hand, trust His heart._

MIND CONTROL

When I am in pain it is extremely difficult to control what goes on in my brain. The pain seems to be in control. Continuing pain makes my nerves feel on edge. It feels like I have surrendered control of my mind and body to the pain. If a sound could be applied to it, the sound of pain in my brain would be similar to the static you hear when a radio is between stations with a few thunderclaps thrown in here and there. A picture of the pain would look something like this: **2hli8tgbhal;df%$^()** **(350aQHFDGTM++_).**

The bold print indicates the intensity of the pain. The lack of space between the figures shows that there is no break in the pain. A lack of organization or sense to the numbers, letters, or symbols is indicative of the lack of sense I find in my pain -- particularly on some days.

Being at peace seems farther from my reach than ever. I read in Isaiah 26:3 trying to discover the secret of that "perfect peace" that is mentioned in that verse. *"You will keep him in perfect peace, Whose mind is stayed on You, Because he trusts in you."* This verse gives a promise of peace -- not just any old peace, but perfect peace. Unger's Bible Dictionary says "perfect" means, *"The fundamental ideal is that of completeness. Absolute perfection is an attribute of God alone. In the highest sense he alone is complete or wanting nothing."* When my brain has been taken over by perfect pain, perfect peace is exactly what I need. Something half-way counterfeit will not get the job done. I need the real thing.

In order to further figure out this verse, we need to sort out to whom the pronouns refer. That first pronoun "You" refers to God. The second pronoun is "him"(or in my case it could be her). That pronoun means the reader or me. So God will keep me in perfect peace. That sounds great to me! I definitely like the sound of "perfect peace" a whole lot better than "perfect pain."

The next phrase, "*Whose mind is stayed on You*" sounds like a condition. "Whose" is another pronoun that refers back to me. It means that I need to keep my mind stayed or fixed on God in order to have His perfect peace. The converse is true. If I <u>don't</u> keep my mind focused on God I <u>won't</u> have that perfect peace. That word "stayed" means "stuck like glue" -- the best super glue ever. I remember how maddening it was when I have gotten my fingers stuck together with super glue. I had to ask my husband to get the nail polish remover just to get my fingers separated. I was a mess! I need to have my mind so stuck on God that nothing can change my focus. That means that even the most awful pain ever won't move my focus from God. I guess perfect peace calls for perfect focus.

The last phrase of the verse tells how maintaining that perfect focus is possible. I know I sure can't do it by myself. "*Because he trusts on You*" is the key. Again we need to examine the pronouns. "He" refers to "me" or the reader. "You" refers to God. In other words, I need to trust in God. In order to have that "perfect peace," I need to trust that whatever God brings across my path is the best thing for me -- even if it is painful. WOW! That is something to chew on for quite a while. I know God is worthy of my trust. He has never let me down. I have just not connected my pain with trusting Him before. God, I trust you even with my pain because I want your perfect peace.

SCARS VS. BEAUTY MARKS

When my oldest granddaughter was 5 years old, it was necessary for her to have a large dark brown birthmark surgically removed from her thigh. Prior to her surgery she called "Grandma" to see what surgery was like because "Grandma" had had more surgeries than anyone she knew. I tried to answer her questions the best I could without frightening her. I told her that she could take a stuffed angel teddy bear I had to the hospital with her to remind her that God had sent guardian angels to watch over her during her surgery. We prayed together over the phone. On surgery day, she was fine as long as she had the angel bear. The birthmark was successfully removed.

This summer, five years after Janie's surgery, we took three of our grandchildren for a swim day at a local recreation center. We had a great time swimming and going down the water slide. While changing clothes my granddaughter was sure some girls across the locker room were pointing at the scar on her thigh. My immediate advice was for her to ignore them, for they were probably too far across the locker room to be able to see her scar anyway.

As we finished getting dressed, 10-year old Janie said, "Grandma, What do you do when people point to your scars? You have more scars than anyone I know." My first reaction was to glibly say that I usually just ignore them. As I looked into Janie's face, I knew the reply she needed deserved more time and thought. I gave her a big hug and we had our own locker room holy huddle.

"When people do ask about my scars or I find them staring, I just explain what caused them. Often answering the questions before they are asked eases the tension. If it doesn't, I ask if they have any other questions. Whether people have questions or point or stare it doesn't change the person I am inside -- the person God made me to be. The acts or questions of others don't change the person God made you to be either, Janie."

I told Janie that there was a person in the Bible who was identified or known by his scars and that person was Jesus Christ. His disciple and friend, Thomas, would not believe that Jesus had risen from the dead until he had placed his fingers into the nail holes (scars) in Jesus hands and feet (John 20:24-28). Jesus appeared and allowed Thomas to identify Him by His scars. Jesus' scars were signs to Thomas of the bad things Jesus had been through and the good that had been accomplished by the bad.

"Janie, when we have scars on our body, it is a sign to other people that we have been through a difficult time. What we need to do is let those people see that our scars are a sign that God has carried us or helped us through those difficult times. Usually scars are thought about as something ugly, or something that makes you look less than perfect. If we can let Jesus shine through our scars so that our scars are marks that identify us with Him, then they become Beauty Marks not just ugly old scars."

PEACE BEYOND UNDERSTANDING

People with disabilities are usually treated differently than "normal people." Some are treated with more courtesy than ever. I got into a museum for free once because I was using a wheelchair. There are some people who become very rude when they come in contact with a person with a disability. They treat a disabled person as if they are too much trouble to deal with. I have had inconsiderate people push in front of the wheelchair, refuse to help with doors, and in general behave in a very obnoxious manner. It is not unusual for people to speak very loudly to someone who is in a wheelchair, as if the disabled person was deaf as well as unable to walk.

Children usually stare, but that is because they don't understand. I always ask children if they have questions. It is usually their parents who are too embarrassed to ask. Once you answer a child's questions, they are fine with the wheelchair and will converse readily. As the child is put at ease the parent is usually more at ease.

It is hard for me to put others at ease with my situation unless I am at ease with it myself. I need to have an inner peace that others can sense whenever they are around me.

That peace needs to be a peace about who I am, about my situation in life, and about my relationship with God. I don't need to have total understanding of my life situation in order to have that peace. I need to trust God with my life.

It would be wrong for me to expect everyone I come into contact with to understand my situation. In order for others to understand my situation, they would have had to walk in my shoes, and I would not want that for them. I would not wish my 6 back surgeries on anyone. I don't want others to have had my health problems in order to understand me.

Philippians 4:6&7 helps a lot. *"Do not be anxious about anything, but in everything, by prayer and petition, with thanksgiving, present your requests to God. And the peace of God, which transcends all understanding, will guard your hearts and your minds in Christ Jesus."* This verse gives us the three-step process which is necessary in order to get the peace which supercedes understanding. Step one is to not be anxious about anything. That is a tall order. It means not to worry about anything, but trust God to handle everything.

The next step is to talk to God about our concerns with thanksgiving because He is always there to help. I don't think it means to be thankful we have concerns, but we can always find something to be thankful about. Things could always be worse. We can be thankful they aren't. The sun keeps shining every day. God does provide for our needs. We need to talk to God about the concerns of our hearts.

Last, but not least, we need to tell God our requests without using God like an internet shopping service. We don't have a no-limit credit account with God. He will see that we have everything we need. He does love us and wants the very best for us. He would not give a 4-year old a new red Porsche because it just would not be appropriate. He can see beyond what we can see. Sometimes we don't understand the answer God gives us. We need to trust in His love to give us what is best for us and let His peace continue to reign in our hearts -- even when we don't understand.

That peace will not only calm our hearts, but according to the Philippians verses, it will also guard our hearts and our minds. I know that my mind needs guarding if anything does. When my mind gets off track, it is hard to tell what sidetrack it will end up on.

Not worrying has some real advantages. Peace is the biggest. Having a "body-guard" for my mind is a great second.

THE BEST IS YET TO COME

"Boy, am I in hot water now!" was an expression my mother used to say when she thought she had done something to displease my father. She knew boiling water would cause great pain. Her statement was a word picture to indicate that she knew Dad would not be happy with her and would probably cause her at least emotional pain.

When cold-blooded animals, such as frogs, are placed in a pot of cool water, their bodily temperature becomes the same as the temperature of the surrounding water. As the temperature of the water increases, so does their bodily temperature.

Boiling water can serve a useful purpose. You can't make a good cup of tea without hot, boiling water. A connoisseur of tea will tell you the pot must be warmed before adding the boiling water for the best possible cup of tea. A tea bag should then steep in the boiling water for about five minutes. Soaking a tea bag in cold water just won't get the job done. The water must be boiling in order to draw out the flavor from the tea leaves, creating the very best cup of tea.

A diamond is a very precious gem. It is difficult to believe it was once a dirty, old, black lump of coal. It takes many pounds of pressure and many degrees of heat to turn that piece of coal into a diamond.

The impurities are brought out of gold and silver ore by the refining process, which involves heat. They are both heated to the melting point and the dross, or the impurities, are skimmed off, leaving the pure metal. With the absence of impurities, the now pure metal is shiny enough to reflect your face.

Some feel we have been through the crucible of refining that has been in the form of physical illness, financial pressures, loss of a loved one, or rebellious children. We have felt the heat of the furnace of public opinion. Joni Eareckson Tada has a good perspective. "When a test heats up, we want to escape; when a trial is pressuring, we want to collapse. If we hold on, remain faithful and rigorously obey, our hearts become refined. Obedience melts away pride and prejudice. Obedience crushes into dust self-centeredness, revealing a heart that is pure and at peace."

Psalms 66:10 says. "For you, O God, tested us; you refined us like silver." The refining process is never fun or pleasant, but it is necessary. God loves us so much. In fact, He loves us too much to leave us the way we are when he knows He can make us to be so much better. It is like a potter throwing a lump of clay on his wheel and making a vase. He then stands back and looks at it from a distance and says. "I can do a better job." He then picks up the clay vase, squashes it, throws it back on the wheel and starts over again.

I have felt the pain of being refined and have not liked it. However, I do trust in God's sovereign wisdom and omniscience (a big word that means He knows everything). When the pain of refinement gets to you and me, we just know the best is yet to come!

MORE THAN A CONQUEROR

Very few families in our country remain untouched by the disease of breast cancer today. It may be a mother, an aunt, a sister, or a daughter who has been attacked by the dread disease. I have a friend who had several lumpectomies leading to a double radical mastectomy. Nearly everyone at least has a friend who has dealt with this threat to their very existence. Most go through at least a bout of depression when they have to decide whether or not they will let the cancer control their lives. The patients who live with it successfully come to grips with the fact that God is in control of the cancer. Those who come to this point are considered "survivors." The survivors can be identified in the Breast Cancer Walks by their pink T-shirts or pink hats.

Joni Eareckson dived into some shallow water as a 17 year old and broke her neck. When her injuries were assessed, it was determined that she would not walk again. She also would not be able to move her body below the shoulders. Joni got a glimpse of God's vision for her life and began Joni and Friends. Joni and Friends is an international ministry to disabled persons and their families. Joni has gone on to sing, paint, and write as she has risen above her disability. Joni is definitely a survivor.

When I was a teenager, my father became mentally ill. The closest cause anyone could figure out is post-traumatic stress syndrome leading back to World War II when he was fighting in the South Pacific. His actions were unpredictable and abusive. I learned protective behavior patterns based on fear rather than love. I transferred these behavior patterns to the way I related to my husband upon my marriage. After Christian counseling and 22 years of marriage, I learned why I felt so secure in these behaviors based on love rather than fear and I, too became a survivor.

I gave my testimony at ladies groups and was told that my experiences and the Scripture verses I had shared with the ladies had been extremely helpful. They said the fact they I admitted to taking an antidepressant gave some of them courage to talk to their doctors about it. Being a survivor was a good thing.

After feeling like I had been a "survivor" for quite some time, I felt like there was something more that I needed to work on. I couldn't imagine another "level," but that is the way I felt. One day I was reading my Bible and I came to Romans 8:35 & 37, "Who shall separate us from the love of Christ? Shall trouble or hardship or persecution or famine or nakedness or danger or sword? … No, in all these things we are more than conquerors through him who loved us."

The conqueror and survivor levels are very different. In verse 37, we are told that we can be "more than a conqueror" or more than a survivor through him who loved us, who is Jesus Christ. Being a conqueror gives one the feeling of getting victory over the enemy. Being a survivor indicates you just "hung on" while something was out of your control. Being "more than a conqueror" makes you the victor and then some because of trust in Jesus strength.

THE MIDNIGHT CRY

My husband is a man of few words and people listen when he speaks. Unlike him, I am a woman of many words. Whether people listen to me or not, sometimes I wonder. The most difficult words I have had to utter in the recent past were the words of final "Good Bye" to my dying mother. She was 83 years old and had only been seriously ill for about six months, but having to say "Good Bye" caused me great pain.

When I was a teenager, Mom and I had our differences, like normal mom/daughter relationships. She didn't like the way I wore my hair and my skirts were too short. However, she was eager to make me a new dress to wear to the school dance. Mom would help me fix my hair so it would look "nice," to her way of thinking. She was trying to be the best mom she knew how to be. We experienced the typical "ups and downs" in our relationship.

After college, I moved out of the state of Ohio. Mom and Dad eventually divorced and Mom moved in with my sister. She continued to live there until the day before she died. Mom tried to help my sister's family with babysitting and housework as long as she was able.

My sister knew Mom was ill when she passed out in church and had to be taken to the Emergency Room by ambulance.

The doctors ran some tests, but could not find the source of the problem, so they turned her over to her family doctor. She passed out a couple more times at home. The doctor put her in the hospital for extensive testing to get to the bottom of the problem. Through all the poking and prodding, Mom was a real trooper. She always said, "I don't care what is wrong. I'm not having surgery. I don't want to be on any machines. I just want to go to Jesus."

It was discovered that the source of her problem was her heart. The left half was only working part of the time and her lungs were filling up with fluid. The only thing that would help was a heart transplant. With her age and general health, that was not really an option. So my sister took her home and tried to make her as comfortable as possible. This worked for a few months.

The time came when my sister, who is a nurse, did not feel that she could leave Mom alone any longer. She called me and said she really needed me to come there and help care for Mom. My sister was having trouble working full-time, caring for her 14- year old daughter, and caring for Mom.

I wanted to help with my mother's care, but that would mean being away from my home and family for an extended period of time I did not have children at home any longer, my boys were grown and on their own. That was not a consideration. The biggest hold-up was that my husband and I had planned to leave for Poland in six weeks for a short- term mission trip with a group from our church. I knew if I went to be with Mom I would not be going to Poland. I tried to talk my husband into going without me. He said that he would not go without me. If I needed to remain in the US because of my mother, then his place was with me. I agonized and cried over the decision and finally decided that if I did not go to be with my mother and she died while I was in Poland I would live with regret the rest of my life.

There were two passages of Scripture that helped me make my decision. The first was Exodus 20:12, *"Honor your father and mother, so that you may live long in the land the Lord your God is giving you."* A similar thought is found in the New Testament in Ephesians 6:2&3, *"Honor your father and mother -- which is the first commandment with a promise -- that it may go well with you and that you may enjoy long life on the earth."*

I went to Ohio to help with my mother's care. Because I did not have the responsibilities of home, work and family I was able to just be with Mom. We would read whatever she wanted. Usually she wanted me to read Scripture or devotional materials. She liked to hear me sing to her. She had favorite hymns like "The Old Rugged Cross" that I sang over and over to her. Sometimes I would just sit and hold her hand. If I had any doubt about whether I was supposed to be there or not, my questions were answered when Mom looked at me with her tired eyes and said, "I like it when you are here."

We talked about what Scripture verses she wanted read at her funeral. She made me promise to have the pastor read John 14:1-4 where it talks about Jesus preparing a place for her in Heaven. She wanted everyone at her funeral to know that she knew Heaven was where she was going and she had no doubts at all. I never thought I would be helping my mother plan her funeral a couple of weeks before her death.

The next two weeks slipped by quickly. Mom seemed to grow weaker almost by the minute. It was becoming increasingly difficult for her to breathe and she was drifting in and out of consciousness. My sister had Mom moved to a Hospice residential facility. Mom was in a coma. Near the end of the day, my sister said she was very tired. I told her I wasn't, so I would take the first watch and she could sleep.

There was a large clock on the wall directly across the room from where I was sitting by Mom's bed. I was sitting holding her hand and singing to her off and on. When she was restless I would sing Christian songs to her. The music seemed to calm her spirit like nothing else. As I watched her labored breathing, I saw the clock on the wall strike midnight, and Mom did not take another breath. I immediately thought of the song "Midnight Cry." One line of the song says, "At the midnight cry, I'll be going home." My mom got a midnight cry and went home to be with Jesus, which was what she had been craving.

I am so glad that I made the choice to be with Mom for her Homegoing and her funeral. Had I been anywhere else the pain would have been unbearable, knowing it had been my choice. I do find great comfort in the fact that I will see her again (I Thess. 4:13-18).

ABC'S OF PAIN MANAGEMENT

A – Always know God loves you. (John 3:16)

B – Bear the burdens of others. (Galatians 6:2) You can reach out to others even if it may only be by phone.

C – Call to ask for moral support or prayer support when you need it.

D – Don't worry about the things of tomorrow. (Mathew 6:34)

E – Every gift we get is ultimately from God (James 1:17). Don't forget!

F – Focus on God and fellowship with friends.

G – Give others the benefit of the doubt when they do not understand your painful situation.

H – Having a sense of humor will put others at ease around you. It will also help you relax.

I – Imagine yourself in Heaven with a body that feels no pain. (Revelation 21:4)

J – Jesus is a friend who sticks closer than a brother. (Proverbs 18:24)

K – Know what real love is. "Jesus Christ laid down his life for us." (I John 3:16)

L – Let friends help you with housework or yard work when you need it because you are all part of the same body.

M – Manage your time so you allow for exercise, rest, and Bible Study, as well as work. Don't feel guilty about time taken for rest.

N – Notice what others do for you and express your appreciation to them with a thank you note or at least a phone call.

0 – Organize your environment as much as possible so you have any adapted equipment or tools you may need close at hand.

P – Prioritize your activities so you get the most important ones finished first. Then if you get tired and can't finish your list, the high priority items will have been completed and the others can wait until the next day.

Q – Question all thoughts which disagree with Scripture, especially those assaulting your own self-worth.

R – Read your Bible and pray daily.

S – Seek medical help including prescription medications as appropriate.

T – Think on things that are excellent or praiseworthy. (Philippians 4:8)

U – Until the day you are healed – don't give up. God is the God of the impossible. (Luke1:37) God may choose to complete your healing in Heaven, but don't give up.

V – Vent your feelings about your pain or your frustrations about being ill to a good friend who can be trusted to keep your confidence.

W – Write down your feelings, helpful Scripture verses, poems, or sayings in a journal. Don't beat yourself up if you don't make a journal entry each and every day.

X – Examine your heart to be sure you have not allowed resentment or bitterness toward God to remain in your heart. This will hinder the working of the Holy Spirit in your life.

Y – Yield yourself to serving God. Don't give yourself over to sin. (Romans 6:13)

Z – Zero in on God's perfect plan for your life. Know that he wants what is good for you and not to harm you. (Jeremiah 29:11)

NOTES

"Never a Discouraging Word:
Ken Caryl Ranch Footprints in Time, Ken Caryl Ranch History Club, 1991 Ken Caryl Master Association, Pages 3, 4

"Pain is a Pain"
Definition of Pain", Webster's New Collegiate Dictionary. G.& C. Meriam Co., Publishers, 1960, page 603

Story of Job – *Holy Bible,* "the Book of Job"

"A Bundle of Potentiality"
Definition of "potential"; Webster's New Collegiate Dictionary, G. & C Merriam Co., Publishers, 1960, page 660.

"The Pain Blanket"
Definition of "chronic"; Webster's New Collegiate Dictionary, G. & C. Meriam Co., Publishers, 1960, page 147

"A Straight, but Painful; Path,
NIV Encouragement Bible; Zondervan House, 2001, page 655

" Disconnected Body Parts"
Hebrews 12:2 from *The Message* translation of the Bible

"Bundle of Potentiality"
Definition of "potential"; Webster"s New Collegiate Dictionary, G. C. Meriam Co. Publishers. 1960, page 660

"God's Big Plan"
Reference to song "Trust His Heart", by Eddie Carswell and Babbie Mason, Causing Change Music and Dayspring Music (a division of Word, Inc.)

All Scripture references are taken from the New International Version of the Bible unless otherwise indicated.

Biography

My father's post-traumatic stress disorder became increasingly controlling and isolating for him and our family. He became very unpredictable. His idea of discipline became a concept of increasing his level of control over my sister and I rather than teaching us how to be productive citizens when we got out on our own. I grew to be very distrustful of male authority figures.

My view of who God is became very warped. I had the idea that my father God was not to be trusted. A very wise Christian counselor convinced me I needed to "risk" trusting God and see what happened. She told me it would be likely that what I would gain by taking the "risk " might be worth it all. I took the "risk" and found that God was loving, gracious, and merciful. I was very glad for my decision.

Following college, I married a great guy named Ken. I nearly exhausted his patience by fearing him as I had my father. Ken had given me no reason to fear him. Overcoming this idea was also accomplished with much counseling, over a period of time.

Ken and I adopted two sons. Like many sons, they went through periods of trying to figure out who they were as young men. This process was compounded by the fact that they were adopted and also needed to answer the question of why their mothers had given them up.

An additional challenge was presented when my doctor informed me that I had developed degenerative disc disease, degenerative joint disease, and fibromyalgia. Chronic pain became a big part of life. Many surgeries have been the result. I asked God to take away my emotional pain as well as my physical pain. He chose not to, but chose to hold my hand and guide me through the combined pain. He taught me how to live in the presence of pain.

I began to write down things I was learning so I wouldn't forget them. The concepts I learned became this book. The most meaningful answers came from the Bible, God's Word.

It is my hope and prayer that these ideas and concepts would be as helpful to others as they have been to me.

I am now living near Denver, Colorado with my husband, Ken and white Maltese dog named, "Moppley". I work very hard in my position as a domestic engineer. My six grandchildren give me great joy. Grandma will baby sit anytime.

Anyone desiring to contact me may do so through my e-mail address, a.m.mcghee@att.net